Animal A[illegible]s

APES

ticktock

First published in Great Britain in 2007 by ticktock Media Ltd.,
Unit 2, Orchard Business Centre, North Farm Road,
Tunbridge Wells, Kent, TN2 3XF

Author: Monica Hughes
Designer: Alix Wood and Emma Randall
Editor: Rebecca Clunes

ISBN 978 1 84696 499 2 pbk

Printed in China

A CIP catalogue record for this book is available from the British Library.

This is Stanley.
Stanley likes apes
and monkeys.

Stanley's mum thinks Stanley
is like a monkey.

Stanley knows a lot about apes and monkeys.

True or False?

Monkeys are apes.

Answers for True or False are on page 32.

Apes and monkeys have lots of hair but Stanley doesn't.

Most walk on their arms and legs but Stanley doesn't.

They are good at climbing but Stanley isn't.

Stanley knows that
chimpanzees are apes.

They live with lots of other chimpanzees.

Their arms are longer than their legs. Chimpanzees are good at climbing.

They are also good at walking on the ground.

They eat fruit, nuts, leaves and **insects**.

True or False?
Some chimpanzees hunt monkeys to eat.

Chimps use tools to help them eat.

Did You Know?

Gorillas don't drink water. They get all the water they need from their food.

Gorillas are African apes.

They live on **grassland**, in woods and in mountain forests.

Gorillas are **vegetarian.**

True or False?

A baby gorilla is about half the weight of a human baby.

Stanley likes the orang-utan
best of all the apes.

Orang-utans are very **rare**.

A male orang-utan lives alone.

A baby lives with its mother for five years.

At night, the mother makes a nest of leaves and branches.

6
5
4
3
Stanley knows that gibbons are the smallest apes.

Gibbons have very long arms.

They are better than the other apes at swinging through trees.

Gibbons live in pairs like a husband and wife.

They stay together all their lives.

True or False?

Gibbons have very loud calls.

BANANA-MILK

This is Stanley's **big** brother.
He is called Lionel.

Stanley thinks his big brother is a bit like an ape.

Lionel is good at climbing.

True or False?

Some apes spend more than five hours a day eating.

He is good at swinging from trees.

He likes to eat and sleep.

Which ape do you think Lionel is like?

He has **ginger** hair like an orang-utan.

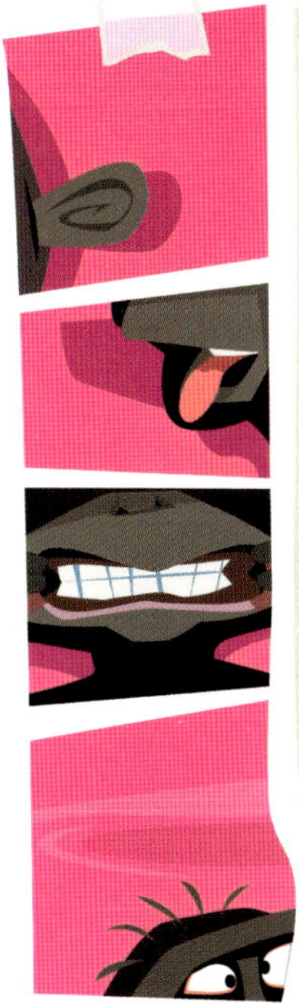

He has long
arms like a
gibbon.

He pulls funny faces
like a chimpanzee.

Stanley's brother is **huge** like a gorilla.

He makes a mess when he is eating like lots of apes.

But Lionel can't make his own bed.
An orang-utan makes a bed in the trees.

Lionel doesn't like vegetables.

Apes eat lots
of vegetables.

Sometimes Stanley does not like his brother.

Sometimes Stanley thinks an ape would be a good brother.

Do YOU think an ape
would be a good brother?

Stanley knows that apes like to share their food.

Do YOU think Stanley would like to share an ape's food?

Stanley knows that apes like to **groom** one another.

Do YOU think Stanley would like an ape to groom him?

Stanley thinks he will keep his brother. Lionel is **big**...

… but a gorilla is even **bigger!**

Glossary

Ginger	A bright orange colour.
Grassland	Dry land with very few trees.
Groom	Pick out dirt.
Insects	Bugs.
Rare	Not often seen.
Vegetarian	Do not eat meat or fish.

True or False answers

Page 4	False Monkeys have tails but apes do NOT have tails.
Page 7	True
Page 9	True
Page 13	True
Page 16	True